Gianni, Jan & Marcello Liscia

WORKBOOK
MOTIVATION

Being ready to perform is the basis for all action

 Illustrations:
Herman Reichold

Motivation is the fifth of five books in the D.R.E.A.M. of LEADERS®
publication series.

Bibliographic information of the The German National Library: The German National Library lists this publication in the German National Bibliography; detailed bibliographic data can be found on the website at http://dnb.dnb.de.

1ˢᵗ edition 2018

Imprint
© 2018 Gianni, Jan & Marcello Liscia

Layout, cover + worksheets: Franziska Eikel, Liscia Consulting
English translation by Ramey Rieger: doitwritetranslations@gmx.de

Text + Layout:
Biographiewerkstatt Böddeker
Ellerstraße 26 – 33100 Paderborn
Telephone: 05293 - 9327816

Print and publishers: : Books on Demand, Norderstedt
ISBN: 978-3-7528-5828-0

Table of Contents

> *"A boss doesn't do the deed,*
> *he awakens the desire to get deeds done."* [1]
>
> Edgar Pisani (French politician)

Dear Reader,

Congratulations! You are now holding *Workbook: Motivation* in your hands, our fifth and final workbook. You are ready to complete your insight into our D.R.E.A.M. Formula and your understanding of leadership.

Should this be your first encounter with us and our books, let us take this opportunity to introduce ourselves. For over 15 years, we have been guiding and promoting people's professional development, an undertaking we carry out with passion. Thus, we have made cultivating leaders our primary responsibility, most specifically, by developing the D.R.E.A.M. Formula[2]:

D Dedication: Wholehearted commitment to mission, 24 hours a day

R Responsibility: Assuming full responsibility for your decisions, for your staff and for yourself

E Education: Ensuring you and your staff evolve

A Attitude: Living and communicating your personal mindset (philosophy) and values

M Motivation: Commitment as the foundation of all deeds

The D.R.E.A.M. Formula acronym can also be understood as a checklist, illustrating the self-concept of a leader. It is how leadership can be understood and lived. This being a highly complex and multi-layered subject, our first publication, *D.R.E.A.M. of LEADERS®. Leadership is not an Illusion*, could only render a first impression of how we understand leadership. Consequently, we have issued a separate workbook for each letter of the D.R.E.A.M. Formula®.

---

[1] Unspecified quotes are taken from *Book of Quotations* (Bassermann-Verlag, 2013) or from digital quote collections.

[2] D.R.E.A.M.-Formel® is a protected trademark owned by Liscia Consulting and registered with the German Patent and Trademark Office.

Our intention is to go further into certain aspects, offer more illustrative examples and provide practical worksheets for you to solidify what you have learned at the end of each chapter. Our workbooks are intentionally designed to be read and applied independently of each other. It is not necessary to read the first book, as the basic structure of the original chapters is the same. We have simply intensified the depth of knowledge with supplementary information and examples.

We usually work with our clients over an extended time period, getting to know one another quite well. Our mission is people work, building relationships, which is reflected in the language we use.[1]

In this workbook, we address the topic *motivation*. We interpret this first and foremost as a leader's willingness to perform. Motivating your employees doesn't mean you should become a cheerleader – much more effective are employee participation, regular two-way communication as well as praise and recognition. The closing chapter goes into the legacy of a leader.

We wish you interesting, refreshing and educational reading!

---

[1] To enhance readability, we have alternated masculine and feminine non-specific personal pronouns per chapter. Hence, in this context, we consider both genders gender-neutral and hope they are understood as such.

M ⌐

Motivation

CEO:	So, you say you're a motivation trainer?
LISCIA:	No, I don't.
CEO:	A motivation coach?
LISCIA:	Nope.
CEO:	You don't show us how to walk over hot coals, beating your breast and shouting, "Whiz-bang!"?
LISCIA:	Definitely not.
CEO:	But you do change your clients lives overnight, right?
LISCIA:	We support our clients in defining and reaching their goals, be they short-term or long-term.
CEO:	Pity. I was looking forward to the hot-coal bit.

Motivation ≠ Cheerleading

When it comes to discussing employee motivation with leaders, they often tell us they would rather not go into it. They feel silly pretending to be cheerleaders. The good news is: that won't be necessary. Motivation has nothing to do with cheerleading or show business.

But we understand very well how this association immediately arises. Just watch the self-proclaimed motivation gurus for five minutes. See them hopping around the stage at their mass events, throwing colorful balls into the crowd or having their followers walk over hot coals. And all the while they rant incessantly, "You can achieve anything! Wealth! Success! The perfect figure! In just one week!" All you need is the right attitude, faith in yourself and, of course, the right guru.

At this point, we have no difficulty bringing our leaders back down to Earth. Motivation has nothing to do with entertainment. No one expects you to swagger up to your employees, throw out your chest and roar them to top performance with breast-beating clichés. That's fast-food psychology, not motivation.

The term motivation is derived from the Latin verb *movere*, and means to move, incite or stimulate toward action. Merriam-Webster.com defines motivation thusly: 1. a) the act or process of motivating; b) the condition of being motivated. 2. a) motivating force, stimulus, or influence: incentive, drive. In our context, motivation means a leader is responsible for guiding employees to discover their own incentive to get somewhere or do something. All the better when combined with cheerfulness, humor and a decent work environment. There's no need to put on a show. In the following chapters, we will illustrate how motivation can be instilled without fireworks or hot coals.

This begs the question: Why are so many people taken in by airy-fairy hype, promising them the pie in the sky? Anyone with a smidgeon of common sense should know that a two-day seminar is not going to prepare them for earning $10,000 a month. Even a child would know that. To prove this points, marketing and business consultant Ben Schulz made a video about this with his two elementary-school-aged daughters.[1] He made them the following offer. If each of them gives him 200€, over the next four days he will teach them everything they need to know so that they never have to go to school again. In only four days, they will learn everything! No more school!

Initially, the girls think it's a great deal. Their eyes light up in anticipation – no more homework, no more tests, no more sitting inside when the sun is shining. Ben, however, asks them to think again. Is it realistic to believe that a four-day seminar will teach them everything they will learn in the next six to eight years of school? The girls only need a few seconds to realize just how unrealistic their father's offer is. Both little girls agree, "That's impossible!" So, if two little kids can figure out what a hoax this is, why do so many people let themselves be jerked around, as Ben so aptly puts it? Why do they pay absurd amounts of money for something they truly must know can't work?

Some people may harbor a glimmer of hope. Maybe it's true? Just like Ben's daughters, who, at first, couldn't wait to get in on the deal. It's like lottery players, hoping against hope that this week their number will hit the jackpot, even though they know full well that the odds of winning are one to 140 million![2] If they didn't have a glint of hope, they wouldn't spend their money week after week on lottery tickets.

Our bipolar instincts are another reason why we allow ourselves to be duped by motivational gurus. On one side is the reward-seeker; you are driven to do

---

[1]   Cf. https://www.youtube.com/watch?v=Hs6kiNUXDIk

[2]   Cf. sueddeutsche.de, *Wie groß ist die Chance im Lotto zu gewinnen? / What are your chances of winning the lottery?* 11.05.2010

something by the anticipation or hope of wealth, recognition, happiness. On the other side is the pain avoidance – the drive to do something in order to deflect negative events such as pain or failure. Alexander Christiani calls this combination of reward and pressure/exertion bipolar instincts, indicating the need to keep both poles in balance.[1] (Read more on polarity in our books *D.R.E.A.M. of LEADERS®. Leadership is not an Illusion* and *Workbook: Responsibility.*)

And this is precisely what we criticize in the overnight sensation promises made by dubious motivational masters – they completely omit to mention the diligence, practice or any other form of personal input involved. They make you believe they have found the ultimate method for becoming rich, famous, successful, slim or, at best, everything at once, without lifting a finger. But we all know that overnight sensations are very rare indeed, and the odds of you becoming one are more or less the same as your chance to crack the lottery jackpot.

Let us say it one more time, loudly and clearly: You can succeed, but it's going to cost you time and effort. Or to quote the German author and comedian Karl Valentin, *Art is beautiful, but it's a hell of a lot of work.*

---

[1] Cf. faz.de, *Morgen mach´ ich es aber wirklich! / Tomorrow I'll do it for sure!* 29.06.2007

Key Lisciaman message
As a leader, you don't have to put on a show to motivate your employees. Don't let yourself be fooled by self-proclaimed motivation gurus. Motivation is more than colorful balls, hot coals and a spectacular performance.

Your notes

Worksheet: What motivates you?

To answer these questions, apply the bipolar motivation model: avoiding disgrace and gaining gusto!

What do you do to avoid or countermand negative input?
What do you do to maintain or gain positive input?
What type are you? A disgrace avoider or gusto gainer? Which side of the model is easier for you to respond to, triggering more thought? Write these thoughts down in the corresponding column.

Avoiding disgrace	Gaining gusto
• Avoiding negative input	• Seeking positive input
• Blocking pain	• Pursuing happiness
• Staving off reproof	• Having fun
• Deflecting reproach	• Striving for rewards
	• Aspiring to recognition

CEO:	We think it's important for our outlet leaders to be role models for their employees.
LISCIA:	My sentiments exactly.
CEO:	That means the boss should always be ready to roll up his or her shirt sleeves and lend a hand.
LISCIA:	Always?
CEO:	Employees shouldn't get the idea that the boss is a snob.
LISCIA:	Can you imagine other options for your leaders to be role models?
CEO:	We've discussed this quite a lot and concluded that pitching in is most effective.
LISCIA:	What about the actual leadership responsibilities?
CEO:	They're a by-product.
LISCIA:	A by-product? The results of your employee survey show, among other things, that your people want more direct, one-on-one feedback. They also want duty rosters scheduled ahead of time, so they can better plan their monthly leisure time activities. So, let's talk about role model functions and by-products again.

Ever-ready to achieve = Leader

A leader must be the vanguard of performance. She is the role model for her employees. Therefore, we understand motivation first and foremost as the leader's willingness to achieve – not to be confused with the *ability* to perform as in the *A.P.F.E.L. Strategy*[1]. (You will find more on our *A.P.F.E.L. Strategy* in our books *D.R.E.A.M. of LEADERS®*. *Leadership is not an Illusion* and in *Workbook: Responsibility.*) Leaders are motivated, willing to achieve 24/7, regardless of how they happen to personally feel that day.

A common argument in this discussion is, "But I can't bend over backward, that's just not who I am." This is our job. Working together with the leader, we discover what her motivating force looks like without putting on a false front. Of course, she should be authentic. Authenticity, however, is not an excuse to stop evolving. There are some men who, during our Business Etiquette Training, insist, "I never wear a tie, it just doesn't suit my personality."

But, especially as a leader, there are situations where a tie is more than appropriate. Naturally, when someone very rarely or never wears a tie, it will

---

[1] The A.P.F.E.L.-Strategie® is a protected trademark owned by Liscia Consulting and registered with the German Patent and Trademark Office.

feel confining the moment he puts one on. So, authenticity or ease in wearing a tie can only be achieved by wearing one every now and then, until it no longer feels alien, but more a part of your person.

The bridge to cross here is the willingness to work on your attitude, which brings us back to changing or evolving. If you are due for a change, then you have to experience or grasp what's in it for you. Wearing a tie can increase your aura of authority when dealing with business partners. It helps you be taken more seriously – or even determine whether you get the job or not. This reminds us of the psychologist Jonas, who lived in our neighborhood a few years. After finishing his studies, he went out looking for a position. Although Jonas had completed university with honors, he could not find a job for the life of him. We were truly surprised until we found out that Jonas went to job interviews in torn jeans, old sweatshirts, poorly-fitting jackets and a five-day beard. He was also a heavy smoker, consuming no less than a pack a day. His fingers and teeth looked it, too.

Still, Jonas couldn't understand why no one wanted to hire him and ranted on and on about superficial employers. "What I'm wearing has nothing to do with my qualifications!" he railed. We tried talking to him, "If you know what personnel expects, then make it easy on yourself. Shave, wear some appropriate clothing and put on a tie." But Jonas didn't want to hear it, "No way! I'm not going to pretend I'm someone I'm not, that wouldn't be authentic!" He adamantly refused to see that some things can't be changed. There are conventions built on certain role models, and these roles are simply mandatory. It's quite possible that Jonas would gradually come to appreciate his new role, allowing it to grow in authenticity. All he had to do was try it out. In time, his good work and strong position in the business, would eventually allow him to write his own dress code.

But Jonas would have nothing to do with it. He declined even thinking about it and categorically rejected our suggestions. He chose to remain authentically unemployable. He holds his head above water with odd jobs, currently working as a lifeguard at the local swimming pool. A certified psychologist! Well, he certainly doesn't have to wear a tie and can remain true to his concept of authenticity…

Praising employees, which we will go into in the next chapter, is also part of motivation. A leader who has not yet learned the fine art of praise, must internalize the importance of a motivating work environment. It may feel strange at first, applauding and praising things that you have thus far taken for granted. But the more often you acknowledge your workers' efforts, the more easily praise will pass your lips as you grasp its power to help you reach your goals.

Besides, this authenticity trend covers only a fraction of who we are. Every human being plays a wide variety of roles in her or his life. – a leader, a shift manager or human resources officer at work; a husband or wife and father or mother at home and a tennis partner during free time. The only essential factor for upholding motivation, is that every role is aligned with your principles.

In our book *D.R.E.A.M. of LEADERS®. Leadership is not an Illusion* as well as in *Workbook: Responsibility* we quoted Stephen Covey, who considers principles the most significant constant in these times of perpetual change. You are quite capable of learning a new role, as long as it essentially concurs with your personality and principles. It's a condition any expectant couple knows quite well. They have no idea what it means to be parents, but they are more than willing to learn.

Accordingly, while first learning a new role, it certainly doesn't feel very authentic. What *does* ring true is your ideal, your striving to learn to *live* the role that is perfectly aligned with your principles. This how you wish to be once you have integrated the role into your being. Otherwise, there is no motivation to assume a new role or function. This is our definition of taking on a new role. It is not play-acting, it is learning.

In educational psychology, this is spoken of as the *four stages of competence*. The first stage is called *unconscious incompetence*, where a person is wholly unaware of her inability to do a certain thing. In the second stage, *conscious incompetence*, she is aware of her ignorance (or, to quote Socrates, "I know that I know nothing") and of the fact that she is lacking the skills to carry out a certain task. In the third stage, *conscious competence*, she has absorbed the knowledge necessary to fulfill the role, but it still costs her effort and concentration to act accordingly. This changes in the fourth stage, *unconscious competence*. She has gathered comprehensive practical experience and integrated the knowledge, body and soul. The skill or role she has assumed becomes second nature and demands little concentration.

An excellent example illustrating the four stages of competence is learning to drive a car. The first few driving lessons fall under the category of *conscious incompetence* (stage 2). This is followed by theoretical and practical learning to attain the necessary knowledge. Once the tests have been passed and the license is in the wallet, you can drive a car, but have to pay particular attention to all the processes involved (stage 3). To graduate to stage 4, you need many hours of driving practice, internalizing the mechanics and training your senses to automatically register what's going on inside and outside of the car.

To become a good leader, or even a D.R.E.A.M. Leader, you must go through these four stages in many areas. It is a constant process that needs a great deal more than one two-day leadership seminar.

This is where Malcolm Gladwell's 10,000-Hour Rule pays off. To achieve outstanding performance, you need to train often and hard. You should also be open to trying out new methods, approaches, etc. A leader must be more than willing to practice, hone and internalize her conscious competence.

(Read detailed information on the 10,000-Hour Rule in our books *D.R.E.A.M. of LEADERS®. Leadership is not an Illusion* and *Workbook: Education*.)

This in turn, affects her authenticity, then conscious competence means she is not yet proficient in all areas. There are skills she is still working on, say, during a transitional process. Some have a problem with this, as their co-workers may notice that something has changed in her leadership style. She worries about losing face or authority when her employees realize she is not completely sure of herself. She's still working on it," may make the rounds.

We consider this a positive development. Leaders are role models and their willingness to achieve is an excellent example of leading the way. If she is not motivated to venture a transitional process, how can she expect her employees to do so? When her co-workers see that their boss is open to learning, they, too, will venture learning. Eventually, learning and evolving will be taken for granted. Besides, losing face is a poor excuse for upholding fallacies that have long been proven utterly dysfunctional. This is especially so in the German culture of errors, which we will talk about more in the next chapter. Presumably, it's much better to stick to the beaten path, putting a good face on a failing situation, instead of admitting a change of course has become necessary. We believe openly and honestly conceding your error or deficit is a sign of strength or sovereignty. We view mistakes or shortcomings as pointers toward learning and evolving.

When speaking of the willingness to perform, the two Formula One racecar drivers Michael and Ralf Schumacher are an excellent example. In 2003, both brothers lined up at the start in Imola for the San Marino Grand Prix, although just that morning they had heard of their mother's death. After the qualification rounds the day before, they had flown their private jet from San Marino to Cologne to pay their final respects to their mother, who then died Sunday morning.[1]

"Michael and Ralf Schumacher achieved the fastest and second fastest time [on Saturday's qualification rounds]. As if they were in a hurry to see their mother one last time. There was no question that they would compete in the next day's race. After winning the qualification round, Michael forbid questions concerning his family. His brother let on, 'Of course, in a situation like this, you wonder if you should race or not. But after the initial shock, it's obvious. You can't just drop everything. No one can.'"[2]

Many people think motivation is walking around with a grin on your face 24/7. Our definition is another. We believe motivation is the willingness to achieve. In 2003, Michael and Ralf Schumacher proved the depth of their professionalism. Yes, their mother had died. Yet, despite this emotional situation, they were also profoundly aware of their responsibility to their respective sponsors, their teams and their fans. Which is why they participated in the race. Although both racing teams gave them the choice not to compete, they competed all the same. Michael Schumacher took first place and even went to the victory ceremony. He accepted the trophy but forewent the customary champagne shower. And

---

[1] Cf. faz.de, *Schumachers starten in Imola / The Schumachers line up in Imola*, 20.04.2003

[2] welt.de, *Bitterer Sieg*, 22.04.2003

that was that. He did not attend the press conference and over the next fourteen days he vanished from public view. Then came the next race, which he also won. This is our understanding of motivation – professionally rising to meet your responsibilities, generating results and fulfilling professional performance expectations, regardless of your personal state of being that day.

A leader most definitely needs strong ego-management or self-management to fully exploit her willingness to achieve. We prefer the term ego-management. Self-management is often mistaken for time-management, although they are two very different concepts. Time-management encompasses administrative and organizational factors, whereby tools such as the Pareto Principle, the Eisenhower Matrix or the ABC method play a significant role in efficiently rostering the many tasks in daily work routines.

Ego-management is a more psychological approach. It is the ability to shape your own personal and professional development, consciously working on yourself and your attitude. A true leader will purposely set aside two or three days whenever the need arises to reflect, perhaps in coaching, on where the weight of her current values lies, or to discover new facets of herself.

Values, as illustrated in chapter *A – Attitude* in our book *D.R.E.A.M. of LEADERS®. Leadership is not an Illusion*, can quite easily change several times in the course of a lifetime. Ergo, they should be regularly updated, changes made conscious and actions accordingly adjusted. (You will find more on the subject of values in our books *D.R.E.A.M. of LEADERS®. Leadership is not an Illusion* and *Workbook: Attitude*.) Are certain values more important to me now than they were two or three years ago? Do these values apply only to my professional life, or to my personal life as well? The update should explicitly concentrate on your singular life, the stuff you are made of, independent of those around you. What is important in your life?

For many leaders, this coaching is both sobering and enlightening as they suddenly realize that there are areas in their lives where they cannot live their most important values. We then analyze together why this is so. Sometimes it simply comes down to not having or making the time for these priorities.

Should this be the case, we explore together how the leader's life could be changed, making space for living her values, shaping the future so she can live

22

in accordance with what is important to her. When you habitually neglect to update your values and to adjust your life accordingly, dissatisfaction and frustration are bound to show their ugly faces sooner or later. Neither of which are conducive to a leader's willingness to achieve.

It was ego-management that also saved Jack's marriage. Jack is a young leader from England who took part in our junior leader program. In his feedback, Jack wrote that his family had always backed him up and been a source of strength, supporting his professional success. This empowering balance between his private and professional life was a constant source of happiness and equanimity. But over the past few years, his focus had gradually shifted more and more toward his work, resulting in less time and energy for his family. Jack didn't notice how dramatically he neglected his family. He loved his job and he and his team enjoyed steady success, so what was the problem? Only when his wife fired a warning shot, speaking of divorce, did Jack realize how far the scales had tipped. When we came to speak of ego-management at the seminar, Jack realized it was time to actually make a change.

Although it was an awkward thing to do, Jack wrote in his feedback, he immediately went to his boss the next day and asked for a transfer to a position within the company which would allow him more time with his family. His boss agreed, but it took nearly another six months before such a position became available. His wife's patience was severely tried, and she began to doubt that her husband was making enough of an effort to save their marriage. This, in turn, intensified the pressure on Jack, who realized how much his family meant to him and how close he had come to losing them.

When he finally began his new job and could gradually bring the areas of his life back in balance, Jack also realized something else. He had won back his empathy, something he hadn't even been aware that he had lost, and the lack of which was wholly alien to his basic values.

Yet, his overwhelming workload had triggered an inability or aversity to listen to his workers when they came to him with issues or suggestions. Only the transfer within the company restored his equilibrium and he was once more able to allow for suggestions and opinions other than his own – an openness he had closed the door on, inch by inch.

A lack of empathy also turned out to be the problem with Viktor, a plant director in eastern Europe. His issue was overzealousness. But let's begin at the beginning. A while ago, Viktor took part in an in-house management development program we carried out at his company. The program included three personal coaching sessions. Viktor's predominant issue was his inability to perform well due to his health condition. It was true. At the beginning of the coaching sessions, he was indeed overweight and sluggish. Although there are countless overweight people with loads of energy, Viktor wasn't one of them. He felt listless and unhappy. It wasn't only how he looked, it was how he felt about himself and his lack of momentum. In our talks, he became aware of how much he had let his health deteriorate over the last years. Consumed wholly with his work as plant director, he had relegated his own well-being to the back seat. This, he wished to change.

Hence, we introduced him to our *A.P.F.E.L. Strategy*[1]. Together, we worked out a plan for improving his eating habits while integrating more physical activities into his everyday routine. The objective was to replenish Viktor's energy levels, generating not only a better self-image but also improving his performance at work, i.e. enhancing his achievement ability.

Viktor was highly motivated to initiate change. In addition to the measures we had worked out together, he hired a personal trainer, working with him several times a week. He soon achieved visible results, which he proudly posted on Facebook, so we could follow his progress as our work at his company was completed. We were happy for Viktor, but after a while noticed he was taking things a bit too far, threatening to topple the whole structure. Viktor had gone from one extreme – practically no physical activity – to the other. His excessive sports gave us cause for worry. Once a workaholic, Viktor had become body-beautiful obsessed, training with the same single-mindedness he once applied to his job.

Viktor had subconsciously transferred his performance principles onto his sport habits, a compensating behavior pattern we have unfortunately observed

---

[1] The A.P.F.E.L.-Strategie® is a protected trademark owned by Liscia Consulting and registered with the German Patent and Trademark Office.

quite often. Combined with professional stress, this behavior is anything but healthy. People have been known to lose their ability to concentrate on their professional responsibilities. In such cases, time is a dominating factor. When, parallel to my demanding leadership responsibilities, I am obsessed with preparing for the next marathon or Ironman competition, I obviously run the risk of neglecting one or the other.

Viktor neglected, and so eventually lost, his empathy. If the man we had initially worked with was a genial, understanding person and boss, he, as we later heard, had taken his hyper-motivation (once focused on his work) to an extreme. His communication and behavior, transferred onto his personal drive to achieve, had made him relentless and, in part, unjust.

Key Lisciaman message
We define motivation essentially as a leader's willingness to achieve. You must be a role model for your employees, forging ahead in performance, regardless of your personal state.

Your notes

Worksheet: The leader as a role model

1. What does being a role model mean to you?

_____

_____

_____

_____

2. What kind of role model would you like to be for your employees? (If you do not have a leading position, then consider for whom you are role model, or would like to be!)

_____

_____

_____

_____

3. Precisely how do you act as a role model?

_____

_____

_____

_____

4. Do you meet all of your own role-model expectations?

_____

_____

_____

_____

5. If not, what can you do to come closer to attaining your role-model-ideals?

_____

_____

_____

_____

CEO:	My staff is already sweating blood when I call them in for a talk. And now you're telling me I should talk to them more often?
LISCIA:	You and/or your predecessor are the reason they're sweating blood. You programed that reaction.
CEO:	What do you mean?
LISCIA:	If the only reason to be called in for a talk is a negative one, it's no wonder your people start panicking at the mere thought.
CEO:	We're not operating a merry-go-round here.
LISCIA:	Well, I have the impression you are going around in circles.
CEO:	What do you recommend?
LISCIA:	Show your employees that a one-on-one can also be for purely positive reasons.
CEO:	And you think that'll work?
LISCIA:	I'm sure of it.

Motivating and inspiring employees

In our books *D.R.E.A.M. of LEADERS®. Leadership is not an Illusion* and *Workbook: Attitude*, we talked about the Book of Happiness. We also pointed out the importance of being attentive to small events. And it is most likely the minor moments leaders notice that motivate their employees the most, inspiring them to perform well. Praising or acknowledging fruitful efforts can work wonders.

"Praise is more effective and has a longer-lasting impact. Co-workers receiving praise set their sights higher, to justify the praise. The brain's biochemical reaction is interesting: Praise causes a flood of dopamine to be distributed, which the brain perceives as a positive event and stores it away in its long-term memory. [...] Motivated and enthusiastic people are more productive, develop better solutions, and radiate positivity, which draws attractive customers."[1]

All the same, leaders are often exceedingly reluctant to praise their employees. "Do I really need to praise and acknowledge things that should be taken for granted? I mean, even tasks that are covered in the employment agreement?" These are frequent questions like that during coaching sessions. And yet, it is the same leaders who expect more from their employees than the contract demands.

---

[1]   zeit.de, *Glück ist ein Wirtschaftsfaktor / Happiness is an economic factor*, 09.01.2015

If the only reward for extra effort is criticism when something goes wrong, you have little right to complain about unmotivated and disgruntled co-workers.

This culture of errors is especially widespread in Germany. An adeptly accomplished task is taken for granted as no big deal, while mistakes are mountains made of mole hills and discussed, deliberated and analyzed to a pulp. When I create a non-appreciative professional environment, i.e. hypercritical, obsessed with control, I inevitably set up barriers, blocking all avenues to success. A negative culture of errors leads implacably to stress, pressure and overextension, smothering in the cradle any resourcefulness or self-initiative.

This is compounded by the fact that 98% of our language usage zeros in on errors. In nearly all of our exchanges, we express negations. We articulate what we don't want instead of clearly describing what we imagine things should be. In our coaching and training sessions, we illustrate this point with a little exercise. We ask participants to close their eyes and listen to the three versions of the following story.

1st version: *It is a beautiful, sunny and mild day. You are standing in front of a large white house with a stunning garden replete with tall trees. A gentle wind rustles their leaves. On the sidewalk in front of the house lies a dog, luxuriously stretched out in the warm sun. As a car drives past, the dog lifts his head for moment.* We now ask the participants what they saw, and they describe the scene as we told it: nice house, wind in the trees, dog on the sidewalk that takes a quick look as a car drives past.

Now we tell them the second version, which begins the same as the first: *It is a beautiful, sunny and mild day. You are standing in front of a large white house with a stunning garden replete with tall trees. A gentle wind rustles their leaves. On the sidewalk in front of the house lies a dog, luxuriously stretched out in the warm sun.* Here, the story changes: *As a car drives past, the dog leaps up and runs after it, barking madly.* When we ask what they saw, our clients said they imagined the dog jumping up and chasing the car, barking madly.

The third version also begins the same as the first and second: *It is a beautiful, sunny and mild day. You are standing in front of a large white house with a stunning garden replete with tall trees. A gentle wind rustles their leaves. On the sidewalk in front of the house lies a dog, luxuriously stretched out in the warm sun.* Once more, the dog's behavior turns the story's plot: *As a car drives past, the dog does not run after it.*

This time, when we ask listeners what they saw, their answers are quite revealing. Most of them imagined the dog didn't move at all, but simply stayed where he was. "But that's not what we said," we respond. "We merely said the dog *didn't* chase the car. So how do you imagine *didn't run?*" This moment always greets us with blank or questioning faces because, of course, it is impossible to imagine *not running*. "What else could the dog have done," we now wanted to know, "could he have walked, crept, jumped, rolled or hopped? These are all alternatives to running. Why do you automatically assume that the dog didn't move at all when we say he didn't run after the car?"

The answer is easy. Since we think in images, our brain cannot process negations. The word *didn't*, doesn't make it to the top shelf. You probably know the pink elephant phenomenon. If you're told not to think of pink elephants, you can't think of anything else.

Now, transfer this insight onto your everyday professional routine. If I tell an employee not to run, then I shouldn't be surprised when he doesn't move at all. Or when one of my workers comes 15 minutes late every day and I tell him, "Don't you dare come in late tomorrow or you're fired." So, on the following day, when the chronically late worker is once more running late, he will call in sick instead of risking losing his job. The actual problem is neither approached nor solved.

His boss should point out the worker's tardiness using a positive formulation, "Make sure to get up 15 minutes earlier tomorrow, so you can be on time for work." Now, the employee has the option to react by taking his boss's suggestion to heart or talking to him. It is also possible that the worker's tardiness has a more complex reason.

A good example is offered by the so-called east Westphalian compliment: After digging into the evening meal, a wife asks her husband how it tastes. He replies, "Not bad." However, his good intentions may be, his wife will not receive this statement as praise or recognition. Since that little word *not* can't be processed, she only really hears *bad*.

And speaking of food, positive language is also very effective, when applying our *A.P.F.E.L. Strategy* if I wish to make dietary changes, I should avoid thinking in taboos. The mere thought of not eating chocolate only triggers a chocolate obsession, making it nearly impossible to stick to my diet. Expressing desires positively is much more effective. Before I begin my diet, I should consider which healthy, tasty (!) alternatives to chocolate there are. Then, when I need a snack, I can enjoy eating something (besides chocolate) with pleasure, not with a guilty conscience.

Excessively upholding a culture of errors and negative language has further drawbacks. If the only reward employees receive for their efforts is negative feedback, they will hardly dare or bother to make suggestions, or offer innovative ideas. Errors or mistakes contain a wealth of positive potential, "Without mistakes, there is no innovation. *Trial and error* is the short and simple watchword. Teflon only came about because a chemist was experimenting with cooling agents and stored them too long. One day, he found white particles coating the insides of the pressure bottle, and voilà – Teflon was discovered. This is but one of a million such stories. So, the next time things go wrong, think of the non-stick frying pan."[1]

We could give even more examples. Scotch tape was another mistake. Initially, the Beiersdorfer Company commissioned their researchers to develop a new tile adhesive. But the material they came up with was too solid. That didn't stop them from putting it on the market as an all-purpose stick-um, which is a given in every office around the world today. The invention of potato chips came about as an act of revenge.

In 1853, every time U.S. American entrepreneur Vanderbilt visited his usual restaurant, he returned his fried potatoes to the kitchen, complaining they still weren't sliced thin enough. The frustrated cook finally shaved them paper-thin and fried them in fat. Instead of being annoyed, Vanderbilt was enthusiastic. Thus, potato chips were invented.

It was pure coincidence when, in 1945, U.S. American engineer Percy Spencer discovered that he could heat up foodstuffs with microwaves. His actual objective was a pipe which later became standard in radar systems. While standing next to his device, he noticed that his chocolate bar was melting. So, he

---

[1] spiegelonline.de, *Macht mehr Fehler! / Make more mistakes!* 08.10.2014

tried out other foods, and it worked! This was the birth of the microwave oven.[1]

Of course, errors must be examined, it's the only way to learn and grow from them. But there must be a balance. A co-worker will much more willingly listen to advice when it is expressed in an essentially appreciative work environment where he is also recognized for his achievements. Without this balance, resistance to criticism and obstinacy are a leader's just desserts.

Thus, it is absolutely critical that a leader maintains a running dialog with his employees, seeking them out regularly. And by this we do not mean the annual, usually obligatory, top-down feedback – a duty which most find tiresome and want to get over with as soon as possible. We recommend a talk at the conclusion of every project, giving leaders an opening for praising his workers, for telling them what an excellent job they are doing and how vital their work is to the company. This recognition must be sincere on all counts. Flattery, or tactical praise, will truly get you nowhere, as it is easily exposed and can just as easily backfire on you.

With sincere praise and recognition, a leader also creates space for approaching those things that are not going so well; space in which employees can evolve. This doesn't always mean a promotion or shift in position. As bizarre as it may sound, not every worker is eager to climb the corporate ladder. (See chapter *E-Education* in our book *D.R.E.A.M. of LEADERS®. Leadership is not an Illusion*)

Nonetheless, it is a leader's duty to foster his employees' continued development, which can just as well take place within a given position. Most people find it gratifying and highly motivating when they see their own productivity improve, fulfilling their assigned tasks even better than before. An annual talk is not nearly enough interaction to gain this end. Conversations on development must be regular items on the agenda, all year round.

Another advantage of regular talks within short intervals is plain and simple immediacy. Neither the leader nor the employee has to dread a lengthy list of mishaps accumulated over the past year, some of which have completely faded from memory. The sooner mistakes are recognized and dealt with, the more

---

[1] CF. stern.de, *Kartoffelchips entstanden aus Rache – sieben geniale Zufallserfindungen / The Potato Chip Revenge – seven brilliant coincidental inventions*, 17.11.2017

efficiently and directly solutions or improvements can be applied to the next project.

This can save you a lot of time, despite the fact that leaders often tell us it is precisely the lack of time that keeps them from talking to their employees regularly. We like to respond by recounting what we were told by a quality manager and his plant director while working together. Both leaders took the time to meet with each of their employees once a week; a direct talk that took from 30 minutes to an hour – every week! They both admitted that it was terribly straining in the beginning, taking up an awful lot of their precious time. Yet, after a while, it paid off doubly, their workers developed remarkably faster and were more motivated on the whole, as well.

The two leaders profited from their efforts. With their employees acting with increased autonomy, they could withdraw somewhat from operative activities, having more leeway for other leadership duties (acquiring new customers, opening new markets, etc.). Investing time in communication and dialog always pays off and also enhances your employees' motivation – not only sporadically, but in the mid-term and long run.

Some leaders confuse positive feedback with a raise in salary. Every worker appreciates more money in his wallet, but it is no substitute for a personal talk, nor for recognition and praise. A padded paycheck must never be the sole form of positive feedback as money alone does not ensure continued motivation. Studies show that recognition for their work and a humane work environment are just as important to employees as a decent salary is. U.S. American businesswoman Mary Kay Ash put this most aptly, "There are two things people want more than sex and money…recognition and praise."[1]

You can easily grow accustomed to extra money. After a few months, the raise is just a given. Much more valuable and long-lasting is the feeling of being seen by those you answer to, knowing they appreciate the work you do day in, day out.

Be proud of your achievements and celebrate your successes! This is a wonderful way to motivate your co-workers. Unfortunately, many leaders have forgotten how to take pause after successfully wrapping up a project; to take time

---

[1]   https://www.brainyquote.com/quotes/mary_kay_ash_148279

for being proud; for appropriately celebrating with co-workers; for enjoying their achievement. We're not talking about a sit-down, 7-course dinner, we're talking about making success – be it a completed project or newly installed software – an occasion to gather your team around you simply in recognition of your joint achievement.

In our books *D.R.E.A.M. of LEADERS®. Leadership is not an Illusion* and *Workbook: Attitude* we spoke about the so-called *reverse gap*. i.e. before new goals are planned, you should pass review of the last few years and ask yourself: What is better today than it was two, three or four years ago? What has changed for the better over this time? What makes me happy today, compared to back then? By focusing on positive past events, you are infused with a sense of happiness, pride and contentment. When I begin to shape my future, I will automatically approach my planning with *reverse gap* awareness; with the knowledge of what is truly important to me and what I wish to carry on into my future.

Taking pause after a successful conclusion is the same idea as the *reverse gap*, a hiatus to take stock of what went well. Giving your co-workers the occasion to take pride in their achievements triggers a flood of positive energy, motivating them to maintain their strong, quality performance.

Key Lisciaman message

Praise and recognition have a positive impact on employee motivation. Add to them positive language usage and regular dialogs, your leadership will create an atmosphere allowing for both mistakes and their resolutions.

Your notes

Worksheet: Praise what is praiseworthy!

When was the last time you praised your employees for specific achievements or qualities? (If you do not hold a leadership position, transfer this exercise onto people in your professional or personal milieu.)

Consider the following aspects:

1. Comportment
2. Attitude
3. Reaching goals
4. Embodying corporate values
5. Job-specific competence
6. Social skills (i.e. exhibits team spirit, is communicative, empathetic and supportive)
7. Practical aptitude (i.e. handling resources such as time, money, materials)
8. Leadership competence (for employees with leadership positions)
9. Personal qualities (i.e. open-mindedness, time management, discipline, quick-wittedness)

Enter your employees' names in the list on the next page and mark the aspects that have earned praise! Follow up with a schedule, denoting when and how you would like to express your praise!

Name	Comportment	Attitude	Reaching goals	Embodying corporate values	Job-specific competence	Social skills	Practical aptitude	Leadership competence	Personal qualities

CEO:	My colleague recently remarked that participation is what you do at a party. She says it has no business on the job.
LISCIA:	Even if such a manipulative misinterpretation of participation were true, I still don't see why there's no place for it at work.
CEO:	For partying?
LISCIA:	Sure. You know, as amusing as it may seem to you, when a leader takes their employees' opinions into consideration when making decisions it is, for the co-workers, something to celebrate.
CEO:	You've got an answer to everything.
LISCIA:	Without question. But let me ask you something: What's your opinion on partying and participation at work?
CEO:	I shouldn't have mentioned it!

Participation is motivating

To enhance your employees' willingness to achieve, or to maintain their high-performance level, they should have as comprehensive an idea as possible of what drives you, their leader. In our books *D.R.E.A.M. of LEADERS®. Leadership is not an Illusion* and *Workbook: Dedication*, we described the significance of a leader's vision and how she should share this spirit with her team, inspiring them to discover their own motivating force.

To do so, it is imperative that they know the destination, know exactly what a new project or transition aims to achieve. They must know their boss's vision and be informed of her strategy. Which market are we approaching? Who is our target group? Which competitors do we have to best? What unique feature are we offering our target group? Tying all this in, objectives are developed to launch these strategies.

The leader must marshal her entire team, perhaps her entire company, behind her. She must equip them to follow her down her chosen road. Her only chance of true success is to share her vision and give her colleagues the opportunity to decide for themselves if they wish to take the journey, carrying their share of the vision to its destination. Is it in alignment with their principles? Do they want the same thing? Do they see the sense in it? If they don't, they will have to change teams, or maybe even leave the company.

We know from experience how often leaders neglect to speak to their employees about why a certain thing is done. But they should. Co-workers are much more willing to do even unpleasant tasks when they know why it should be done. The terse, "That's what I pay you for!" has understandably little motivating force behind it. Your employees want to and must know which bigger picture their efforts are serving to assemble.

Participation, however, is not only a mere passing on of information. It is also listening to employees' ideas (*open innovation*) and/or giving them the chance to participate in decision-making. In this context, Ken Blanchard and Spencer Johnson speak of the *participative leadership* concept in their book *One Minute Manager*[1]. It is highly motivating for an employee when her suggestion is considered, and it leads to process or product improvement.

"Looking at Audi clearly illustrates how those involved know what is best for themselves and their product. [...] ›When, for example, upon developing a model, the cup holder is installed too close to the gear box, open innovation can remedy such an error much more quickly. ‹, Oliver Schilling, Audi organizational developer says."[2]

We sincerely hope the worker catching and correcting this error received proper praise from her boss, inspiring pride and continued eagerness to perform well. No less impressive than admitting a mistake, a leader demonstrates her surety when she can sincerely exclaim, "Many thanks, Mr. Miller, we completely overlooked the proximity to the gear box." Subsequently, she couldn't dream of a more motivated co-worker – Mr. Miller will gladly continue to participate in fulfilling the vision.

Still and all, the leader must always have the last word. She mustn't run around, pretending to listen to and earnestly consider any and all suggestions. Many suggestions, regardless of their basic viability, are doomed to fail because their implementation is too costly. And this the leader's responsibility. She must ensure that her decisions are always in the company's best interest. Participative leadership is *not* a democracy. There is no majority rule.

There is yet another plus side to having well-informed employees. They will

---

[1]   Blanchard, Kenneth etc., *The One-Minute Manager*, Berkeley Trade 1986

[2]   sueddeutsche.de, *Uns fragt ja niemand! / No one bothers to ask us!* 05.06.2011

be more inclined to persevere through challenging times because they know exactly why they're doing it. In this context, we find the reference to *salutogenesis* worth-while. The term was coined by Aaron Antonovsky, a professor of medical sociology, and deals with the origins of health, as opposed to the origins of disease, known as *pathogenesis*.

In the 1970s, Antonovsky examined the characteristics and resources that helped people maintain their physical and psychological health, even after suffering the most debilitating situations. In a nutshell, Antonovsky's findings culminated in what he called a *sense of coherence*, a quality that contributes most to deflecting health risks. This *sense of coherence* is composed of three factors - *meaningfulness, comprehensibility* and *manageability*.[1]

We have already covered the first two factors referring to motivating co-workers. Only when their work is meaningful; when they are party to decision-making processes, can they fulfill their leader's expectations. Also decisive is Antonovsky's *manageability*, defined as how a person, despite the physical and emotional burden of today's working world, can face her challenges with a determined, "I can do it!"

And this desired condition is only possible when employees have the required physical and psychological resources, as previously delineated in the *A.P.F.E.L. Strategy*, and for which the leader is responsible. If stamina and performability are not maintained, the willingness to achieve will also fall into disrepair.

As a leader, I owe it to my team to create a positive atmosphere. A place where they feel they have access to enough resources to fulfil their assigned tasks. It is nearly impossible to avoid stress in our modern working world, but when Antonovsky's three factors are accounted for, your employees will be able to handle the pressure. Especially if they are working in a fundamentally supportive environment where they absorb more positive eustress, energizing instead of exhausting them.

Another aspect of *manageability* is integrating positive experiences. When I have, for example, successfully passed through a difficult professional situation, I come out motivated for the next challenge, knowing I own the

---

[1] Cf. Petzold, Theodor Dierk, *Praxisbuch Salutogenese. Warum Gesundheit ansteckend ist / Why Health is Infectious*, südwest 2010. English reference: https://en.wikipedia.org/wiki/Salutogenesis

necessary resources to master it. Think of the *story changing*® *board's* 12th step (See *D.R.E.A.M. of LEADERS*®. *Leadership is not an Illusion* and *Workbook: Responsibility*): The conclusion of a transition is also the moment to begin the lessons-learned process; to reflect on what went well, or not so well, and what to keep in mind for the next project.

Jana provides us with an excellent example of what happens when the factors as defined by Antonovsky are neglected. When our client, a retail furniture chain, introduced us to their new brand and product manager we were immediately taken with her boundless energy and originality. She had delightful communication skills, easily establishing relationships. Jana was also highly qualified, and we congratulated our client on finding such a valuable new colleague.

The joy was short-lived though, as Jana rescinded her contract with the company only five months into her trial period. How could that be? To better understand the situation, we need to first give you some background on the company's development. Somewhat over ten years ago, the company began with eight showrooms throughout Germany. The initial target group was commercial customers seeking high-end, quality office furnishings ranging from customized conference tables, desks, sofas and chairs to shelves and cupboard systems. Over time, the company was furnishing not only hotels, home offices and businesses all over the world, they also equipped ocean liners and restaurants.

About seven years ago, company executives decided to expand the business, targeting private customers as well. To this end, approximately every two years, nation-wide concept stores were opened, serving specific target groups. The first concept store dealt in Scandinavian furniture. Two years later came the concept store for Mediterranean Living, which after two years was followed by Kitchen Stores. The company is currently working on a concept for discount furniture warehouses with drive-in services for large cities.

All concepts are running smoothly to date and profits are good. Yet every new development costs time and energy, in part because company leaders get bogged down in details, neglecting to keep the original concept up to date. Developments stagnated, and employees were kept at arm's length, left to waste away. This is where Jana comes in. She was explicitly hired to nurse the orphaned high-end segment back to health. As brand and product manager, the high-end concept was her sole responsibility, and she was perfect for the position, both professionally and personally.

But her leader failed to lead. Over the next months, Jana made countless suggestions, but was left hovering in a vacuum. She received neither comment nor criticism on her ideas. As there were no decisions made, she was unable to take decisive action. Jana eventually realized the futility of her efforts (meaningfulness); she witnessed the utter lack of manageability devour her motivation – two of the three *salutogenesis* factors died. If you never receive feedback, you can never know if your efforts are moving in the desired direction or not. So why bother to make suggestions at all? It's a waste of energy, and each new fruitless attempt is another blow to motivation. Jana did not have the authority to make decisions, which wiped out her manageability, leaving her no other choice than to wonder just how much leeway she actually had. What impact *could* she have, what *could* she achieve? Realistically? None and nothing.

This brought the inherently optimistic, go-getter brand and product manager down to earth. She ultimately chalked it up to experience and resigned, which we found completely in character. Jana was someone who knew where she was going. She was, and is, fully capable of making objective-related, critical decisions and implementing them responsibly. Since her employer stymied any possible developments and she saw no prospects of this changing any time in the future, she did the only self-respecting thing – she left the enterprise before the end of her trial period. From her point of view, this was her only option.

For the furniture chain, Jana's departure was a bitter loss. She was most certainly capable of refurbishing the original concept, infusing it with new impulses. She also would have rejuvenated the languishing employees, giving them new purpose. None of this came about because Jana received the same cold-shoulder treatment; no decisions were made. Our client is now in the same dilemma. The original concept lays stagnating. They have yet to find a replacement for Jana, such high performers are few and far between.

Unfortunately, Jana is not a singularity in this corporation. In fact, it seems to have become a recurring phenomenon: Executives decide to push a certain concept or personnel development, occasionally even hiring someone for the job. But the moment that person takes up her responsibilities, she is completely ignored. Regular dialogs, the significance of which we illustrated in the chapter before last, just don't happen. We know of another employee who left this company after years of service because his employer only met with him once a year, their talk lasting a matter of minutes and touched on nothing of importance. This highly competent, initially deeply motivated employee, who contributed clever ideas, repeatedly appealed to his boss for feedback talks. If an appointment was finally set, his boss would cancel the meeting without explanation. When this man discovered that he hadn't spoken to his boss in over a year (!), he resigned. His efforts for the company had been thwarted one too many times.

Naturally, we approached our client with appropriate feedback, impressing upon him his negligence in allowing such desirable employees to leave the company. Particularly in these times when skilled workers are scarce, companies should do all they can do to encourage and advance their engaged workers, giving them good reason to be loyal. But, much to our dismay, some leaders are advice-resistant...

This also applies to another of our clients, a globally active corporation on the metal-working sector. Some three years ago, we established a Manager Development program there, working under the premise, "Our plant managers must be trained to make more independent decisions." The plant managers themselves were thrilled by the concept. Their motivation had long been suffering under the lack of leeway their employer allowed, taking the meaningfulness out of their professional existence. The corporation, however, only applied the skeleton of our concept, without noticeably expanding plant managers' leeway. The space afforded them to act independently was carefully measured out – so far and no further. All other decisions were made two or four levels higher, without asking for, so not hearing, their input.

One plant manager refused to play along and resigned his position. A loss we viewed as catastrophic, this was a man to hold on to at all costs. Still today, we consider him the prototype D.R.E.A.M. leader, capable of developing and inspiring his employees, making them a part of his vision. He is also a highly skilled manager, creating and maintaining well-oiled processes and systems. When speaking with us, the plant manager expressed his unwillingness to continue working on such a tight leash. With so little freedom to make decisions, he simply cannot summon the motivation to carry on. We understood completely!

In contrast, one of our coachees, Bernd, had all the freedom in the world at the logistic enterprise where he worked. This enabled him, over six or seven years, to develop from design engineer to vice president of project management. Arriving at the top, where his only superior was the executive board, Bernd no longer had the freedom that had so motivated him when he was further down in the hierarchy. Disappointed, he resigned from the company and became an independent consultant, hoping this would bring him the desired personal initiative. His objective was to advise businesses on defining and implementing project management.

After a time, Bernd felt his clients' resistance to his advice and experienced what we know all too well. As a consultant, you can develop the most brilliant concepts and make effective suggestions, but the client will always have the final word. At the end of the day, it is the client who will decide what to implement and what to table. Ergo, the greater impact Bernd was hoping to have as an independent just wasn't going to happen. This meant his desired manageability also deflated in disappointment. Bernd then took on a position in a globally active accountancy and consultancy firm as department manager. But this company was not quite ready for the changes Bernd hoped to initiate, causing his manageability to once more fall flat.

So, our coachee once more changed employers. Here, he was able to satisfy both his need for self-efficacy and his need for manageability and remained with this company for several years. At some point, Bernd realized he had done all he could do in this position. He left the company and returned to the accountancy and consultancy firm, which had successfully brought a years-long transitional process to a close. The conditions were now those Bernd had desired years ago, satisfying his manageability drive.

This is a good example of a person who is not solely interested in career, money or security. Bernd's motivation is, was and has always been drawn from participation. He wants to be a part of decision-making processes, to make an impact and thereby put processes in gear and watch them roll out. If an employer does not provide these parameters, Bernd does not hesitate to leave the company in search of new challenges.

Key Lisciaman message
Participative leadership is vital to employee motivation. The three factors, meaningfulness, comprehensibility and manageability are also significant to long-term motivation.

Your notes

46

Worksheet: Checklist for three important motivational factors for both you and your employees

Fill out the checklist for you and your employees, describing how the three factors are fulfilled to enable an elevated level of motivation! If you do not hold a leadership position, fill out the check list for yourself and others in your professional/personal milieu!

1. Meaningfulness – seeing the point or value in your work
2. Self-efficacy – options for influencing your activities
3. Manageability – possessing the physical and mental resiliency to meet your responsibilities

Name	Meaningfulness Fulfilled how?	Self-efficacy Fulfilled how?	Manageability Fulfilled how?
Me			

> | *CEO:* | You know, throughout all these decades of my professional life, I have spent the most time and energy passing on my business acumen to my employees. My priority has always been, and always will be, to hold our work at the highest level, improving it whenever and wherever possible. As I grow older, with only another ten years before I retire, I become increasingly aware of something else I must hand down to the younger generation. They need to know more than professional skills and expertise if this enterprise is to remain successful in the coming decades. |
> | --- | --- |
> | *LISCIA:* | And what is this something else? |
> | *CEO:* | How to lead. |
> | *LISCIA:* | Well said. |

The legacy of a leader

At a certain salary level, money is no longer a motivator. It is merely, as the U.S. American professor Frederick Herzberg so aptly put it, a *hygiene factor*.[1] His fellow countryman, the psychologist and entrepreneur Richard A. Chaifetz, described it thusly, "Money is only a by-product of success." So, what is the main product? What motivates a leader beyond his annual income and bonuses?

At the beginning of his career, it is the aforementioned visions, his clear future outlook that drives him on to achieve. Later on, as the end of his professional life comes into view, a leader will ask himself what mark he has made. What is his leadership legacy?

He would like to look back and know he has left behind something beyond material value, something ideational. We are familiar with the legacy of politicians. Take Helmut Kohl (1930-2017), known as the *Chancellor of Reunification*, or Barack Obama and his slogan *Yes, we can!* Both of whom will go down in history.

The shape or perception of such a legacy is as unique as the one creating it. Just compare Microsoft founder Bill Gates and Apple initiator Steve Jobs: "There are a number of myths and legends surrounding Bill Gates himself, but

---

[1]   Herzberg, Frederick, *One more time: How do you motivate employees*, Harvard Business Review Jan./Feb. 1968

his corporation has no particular vision. That's quite different with Apple. Jobs basically never did anything else besides building and selling computers[...]. But *how* he did it, his vision, welded the trademark Apple to his name. Ten years ago, Bill Gates resigned as Microsoft chairman of the board [...]. No big deal. When [...] Steve Jobs became seriously ill 2 years ago, the market, customers, fans and media were all in a panic. [...] Hardly anyone could imagine it – Apple without Jobs."[1]

But they had no choice. When Jobs died on October 5, 2011, he not only left behind a multi-billion-dollar business, he had made his mark by revolutionizing the digital world. Earning money was apparently not a primary objective, "I had over a million dollars when I was 23 years old; over 10 million when I was 24, and more than 100 million at 25 – and I could have cared less, because I didn't do it for the money."[2]

Striving to create a legacy is yet another attribute separating leaders from managers. Particularly managers who go corporate-hopping at breakneck speed and often don't give a damn that they leave nothing but burned rubber behind them. The past years have seen some severe public criticism on this issue, and it is justified. Especially in view of the inalienable bonus or indemnity running into the millions, even for managers who leave their concern or bank in economic ruins and/or with a shattered reputation, as in the recent emissions scandal in the automobile industry. Such managers are only interested in what's in it for them, to hell with ideational legacies. They are nothing more than monstrously overpaid clock-punchers. There are black sheep in every profession, and we by no means wish to sully the name of manager in general. All the less so since there are people who – technically speaking – fulfill our D.R.E.A.M. Formula but do not even come close to being *leaders* as their visions are those of destruction. Every dictator is also driven by a clear view of the future, but their visions are lightyears away from honorable…

An ideational legacy can also take the shape of social engagement. Dietmar Hopp, co-founder of SAP, sponsored the soccer club *1899 Hoffenheim*, a club he played for in his youth, with 350 million euros, enabling the club to move

---

[1] brandeins.de, *Das Vermächtnis / The Legacy,* issue 09/2010

[2] Cited from the 1996 TV documentary *Triumph of the Nerds.*

from the regional league to the national league between 1990 and 2008. Social projects are even more important to Dietmar Hopp than soccer. He donates lavishly, predominantly in his home region, as, in his own words, he is "… deeply indebted to the people there."[1]

For Facebook founder Mark Zuckerberg, gratitude also inspires generosity. Following the birth of his daughter, he announced his intention to donate 99 percent of his Facebook shares to charity, amounting to 45 billion dollars.[2] These are but two examples of leaders' legacies.

A leader who has dedicated his entire professional life to feeding the fire of his vision, also burns to pass the flame of his passion on to the next generation. As the Austrian composer Gustav Mahler once said, "Tradition is not the worship of ashes, but passing down the fire."

When we speak of the legacy of a leader, a crucial facet is the ability to shape other leaders, who, in turn, are equally capable of kindling the leadership spark. Not only transferring knowledge and expertise – which is all well and good – but a leader should be able to teach others how to lead. In this way, his legacy is passed on when he leaves the company or ends his professional life. His visions will be carried on…

To discover what your legacy could be after you retire from your professional life, self-management often draws on the *alien assessment* technique. Usually, this a eulogy and the assigned question is, "When someone gives a funeral oration at my grave, what would he say? What would this person believe to be my personal achievements or my legacy?"

We steer away from the morbid eulogy and adapt the exercise to a more positive, less final scenario. Your assignment is to write a speech from a colleague's point of view, to be given at your retirement party. The speech refers primarily to your professional career. The primary focus, however, is not on the colleague's assessment, it's major theme answers the question, "How does this person believe I see myself?" This question; this assumed self-evaluation is where

---

[1] Cf. zeit.de, *Fußballclubs sollten drei Prozent für Soziales geben / Soccer clubs should donate three percent to charity*, 04.01.2017

[2] Cf. spiegelonline.de, *Zuckerbergs Weltverbesserungsdings erlöst 95 Millionen Dollar / Zuckerberg's World Improvement Tick Donates 95 Million Dollars*, 23.08.2016

things get really interesting. It is not only a question of how well your colleagues or superiors know you, or believe they know you, but how well they know how you think about yourself. This change of perspective reveals a completely new view of what my legacy looks like, of the mark I wish to leave on this world, or in this case, on my company (my department, my team) when I retire.

Key Lisciaman message
Money is not the only motivator for a leader. You would like your efforts to also leave an ideational imprint, be it social engagement or a legacy of strong leadership.

Your notes

_____
_____
_____
_____
_____
_____
_____
_____
_____
_____
_____
_____
_____
_____
_____
_____
_____
_____

Worksheet: The final farewell

Imagine we travel in time to the day of your retirement. At your farewell reception, either a good friend, a colleague, a long-term employee or your superior gives a speech about you, and only about you. What would this person say about you – as a person, colleague and leader? Write this speech from their point of view!

The Authors

Marcello, Gianni and Jan Liscia (left to right)

Since its inception in 2000, taking shape in Paderborn, Germany, the name *Liscia Consulting* has gained ground on both national and international terrain with their excellent work in leader development. A most competent partner for strategy, conception and getting things done.

Business leaders Gianni, Marcello and Jan Liscia are not your everyday seminar conductors. Nor are they generic trainers or coaches. Gianni, Marcello and Jan Liscia are consultants who train and coach *leaders*. They are strategic partners, guiding and mediating transitional processes.

www.Liscia-Consulting.com

Keynote presentations for your event

On the pulse of change with inspiring keynote lectures! A keynote presentation can be designed to run 30 minutes or up to 3 hours – according to your event's agenda!

Together, we determine the focus of your D.R.E.A.M. of LEADERS® keynote lecture, i.e. Employee Engagement in Global Leadership, Transitional Process Leadership or Digital Leadership. Our multifarious and unusual approach infuses your business with new impulses, creating an atmosphere of awakening and a desire for change.

A rational/emotional composition coupled with the blunt, stark reality of our times invokes profound reflection. To easier digest discomfiting truth, we served it with a healthy portion of humor.

www.Liscia-Consulting.com

One 'n' Herman, the artist

Herman, illustrator

Herman is, and has been for some time, one of the most high-profile, successful pop art painters of our time. His edgy, idiosyncratic graphics and pictures are downright bodacious. Once a trained screen printer, his unleashed creativity has astonished viewers at over 200 national and international exhibits. Herman has been an independent artist since 1991.

Over the past years, the name Herman can also be found under cartoons drawn for a variety of German publishing houses. His *flying heart* comic strip in *Bravo*, a German youth magazine, was published several consecutive years, becoming a household name. The same can be said of the 18 Herman collector's glasses commissioned by *Ritzenhoff*. In 2007, bids were made for 49 Herman paintings at a charity auction benefiting the Peter Maffay Foundation.

www.Kuenstler-Herman.de

**Want more? Here's an overview of all books
by Gianni, Jan & Marcello Liscia:**

Gianni, Jan & Marcello Liscia

D.R.E.A.M.
of
LEADERS

Leadership is not an Illusion

Illustrations:
Herman Reichold

ISBN: 978-3-744-88271-2 – 19,90 € (D), E-Book: 14,99 € (D)

Gianni, Jan & Marcello Liscia

WORKBOOK
DEDICATION

Dedication to the work at hand, with heart and soul,
24 hours a day

Illustrations:
Herman Reichold

ISBN: 978-3-7528-5787-0 – 8,90 € (D), E-Book: 4,99 € (D)

Gianni, Jan & Marcello Liscia

WORKBOOK
RESPONSIBILITY

Showing responsibility for decisions made, for employees
and for oneself

Illustrations:
Herman Reichold

ISBN: 978-3-7528-5825-9 – 8,90 € (D), E-Book: 4,99 € (D)

Gianni, Jan & Marcello Liscia

WORKBOOK
EDUCATION

Personal and employee education

Illustrations:
Herman Reichold

ISBN: 978-3-7528-5826-6 – 8,90 € (D), E-Book: 4,99 € (D)

Gianni, Jan & Marcello Liscia

WORKBOOK
ATTITUDE

A question of personal attitude and values which are
lived and experienced

Illustrations:
Herman Reichold

ISBN: 978-3-7528-5827-3 – 8,90 € (D), E-Book: 4,99 € (D)

Gianni, Jan & Marcello Liscia

The Book of Happiness

A work and reflection diary

Illustrations:
Herman Reichold

ISBN: 978-3-7528-5829-7 – 8,90 € (D)

All of our titles are available as ebooks (except The Book of Happiness) and can be enjoyed in the German language, too!